LITTLE WHISPERS OF ENCOURAGEMENT

for Girls

LITTLE WHISPERS OF ENCOURAGEMENT
for Girls

BARBOUR
PUBLISHING

I will love You,
O Lord, my strength.

Psalm 18:1 NKJV

YOU ARE GOD'S PRECIOUS CREATION.
THANK HIM FOR LOVING YOU.

take time every day
to do something silly.

PHILIPS WALKER

Stay true to your word:

Keep your promises.

Encourage Others—
Lend a helping hand.

God gave you a gift of 86,400 seconds today. Have you used one to say, "Thank you"?

William A. Ward

How beautiful a day can be
when kindness touches it.

GEORGE ELLISTON

Relax a little.
take time to daydream.

ENCOURAGE OTHERS—
SHARE YOUR FAITH THROUGH YOUR DAILY
ACTIONS.

LIGHTEN UP!
LAUGHTER IS THE BEST MEDICINE.

Pray every day.
You'll be glad you did.

Be happy for others.

Don't be concerned about the outward beauty of fancy hairstyles, expensive jewelry, or beautiful clothes. You should clothe yourselves instead with the beauty that comes from within. . . which is so precious to God.

1 Peter 3:3–4 NLT

When you are faced with indecision, pray. God will lead you in the right direction.

Walking with a friend in the dark is better than walking alone in the light.

HELEN KELLER

INCLUDE EVERYONE;

NO ONE WANTS TO BE LEFT OUT.

The Lord has great plans for your life.
Thank Him in advance.

THE LORD'S LOVE IS EVERLASTING
AND ETERNAL.
TRY TO FOLLOW HIS AMAZING EXAMPLE.

No need to worry.
God will fulfill all your needs.

PEOPLE CAN SEE GOD THROUGH YOUR ACTIONS.
WHAT IMPRESSION ARE YOU LEAVING BEHIND?

It's not that you won or lost. . .

but how you played the game.

Grantland Rice

ENCOURAGE OTHERS—
SURPRISE YOUR PARENTS WITH A
HOMEMADE CARD OR GIFT.

No need to ever be afraid.
God will protect you
with His almighty love.

Learn to laugh at yourself.

LET THE WORDS OF MY MOUTH
AND THE THOUGHTS OF MY HEART BE
PLEASING IN YOUR EYES, O LORD,
MY ROCK AND THE ONE WHO SAVES ME.

PSALM 19:14 NLV

THE LORD TEACHES US LESSONS TO HELP

US MAKE BETTER DECISIONS FOR OUR FUTURE.

Alone we can do so little;
together we can do so much.

HELEN KELLER

When life is hard, pray.

RESPECT OTHERS—

NO IFS, ANDS, OR BUTS.

Jesus will be your friend until the end.
He'll never leave you lonely.

A laugh is a smile that bursts.

Mary H. Waldrip

Choose to be happy.

YOU CAN'T WRAP LOVE IN A BOX, BUT YOU CAN

WRAP A PERSON IN A HUG.

UNKNOWN

GOD IS INCREDIBLE.
BE THANKFUL THAT HE LOVES YOU ENOUGH
TO OFFER YOU LIFE THAT NEVER ENDS.

You are a child of God.

You'll make mistakes in life.
Learn from them.

"You are the light of the world.
Let your light shine before men, that they
may see your good deeds and praise
your Father in heaven."

Matthew 5:14, 16 niv

You don't always have to be first in line.
Let someone else have the opportunity
to be first once in a while.

Don't look down on anybody.
Instead, reach down and help people up.

Take a few minutes to thank God for
His precious love and blessings.

START YOUR DAY OFF RIGHT: PRAY BEFORE
YOU CRAWL OUT OF BED IN THE MORNING.

ALWAYS BE A FIRST-RATE VERSION OF
YOURSELF, INSTEAD OF A SECOND-RATE
VERSION OF SOMEBODY ELSE.

JUDY GARLAND

You are always safe in God's hands.

Learn when to have fun and when to be serious. there's a right time for everything.

Encourage Others—
Spend the weekend enjoying a new
activity with your friends.

Before you put on a frown,
make absolutely sure there
are no smiles available.

Jim Beggs

Be thankful.
God has given you *so* much.

Giving is better than receiving.

ALWAYS DO YOUR BEST TO
MAKE GOD HAPPY.

"Don't be afraid, for I am with you.
Don't be discouraged, for I am your God.
I will strengthen you and help you."

Isaiah 41:10 NLT

Kind words can be short and easy to speak, but their echoes are truly endless.

MOTHER TERESA

If you are afraid, Jesus will give you the courage to keep going.

FIND A QUIET PLACE TO PRAY AND THANK
GOD FOR THE WONDERS OF THE DAY.

This is the day the Lord has made;
let us rejoice and be glad in it.

PSALM 118:24 NIV

IF SOMEONE DOES A FAVOR FOR YOU,

BE SURE TO RETURN IT.

SMILE. IT'S CONTAGIOUS.

Give your worries to God.
He wants you to!

THE TIME IS ALWAYS RIGHT

TO DO WHAT IS RIGHT.

MARTIN LUTHER KING JR.

Everything is more fun when
you're with a friend.

Enjoy the beauty God has
created around you.

GOD'S TIMING MAY NOT BE AS
FAST AS YOU'D LIKE, BUT HE KNOWS
WHAT IS BEST FOR YOU.

A BIRD DOESN'T SING BECAUSE IT HAS AN
ANSWER; IT SINGS BECAUSE IT HAS A SONG.

MAYA ANGELOU

No problem is too big for God.

FOR IF A MAN BELONGS TO CHRIST,
HE IS A NEW PERSON. THE OLD LIFE IS GONE.
NEW LIFE HAS BEGUN.

2 CORINTHIANS 5:17 NLV

WHEN YOU TELL GOD, "SORRY,"
HE WILL FORGIVE YOU IMMEDIATELY AND
WRAP YOU IN HIS EVERLASTING LOVE.

There is a time for everything,

and a season for every activity under heaven.

Ecclesiastes 3:1 NIV

Real beauty shines
from the inside out.

No matter what happens,
Jesus will always love you.

TELL YOUR PARENTS YOU LOVE THEM—
TELL THEM OFTEN.

GOD HAS THE PERFECT LIFE FOR YOU.
TRUST HIM, AND HE'LL GIVE YOU MORE
THAN YOU EVER DREAMED POSSIBLE.

God knows what is best for you.
He will provide for all your needs.

when in doubt, tell the truth.

MARK TWAIN

Encourage Others—

Share what you have with someone else.

BE COURAGEOUS—

STAND UP FOR YOUR BELIEF IN JESUS.

God will handle any problem you
have because He loves you.

Giving is true loving.

CHARLES SPURGEON

IF YOU HURT SOMEONE, BE QUICK TO SAY,
"I'M SORRY."

Do not lose the dreams of today
because you are too focused on
your journey toward tomorrow.

God gave you many wonderful gifts.
Use them to glorify Him.

No dream is too big when
you have faith in God.

GOD MADE YOU UNIQUE.
THANK HIM FOR HIS HANDIWORK.

Encourage others—
treat others the way you would
like to be treated.

ACT AS IF WHAT YOU DO MAKES
A DIFFERENCE. IT DOES.

WILLIAM JAMES

Stay true to your word.
Keep a secret.

GOD IS BY YOUR SIDE, EVEN WHEN
YOU'RE FEELING TEMPTED.
PRAY, AND HE'LL BE THERE TO RESCUE YOU.

"WITH GOD ALL THINGS ARE POSSIBLE."

MATTHEW 19:26 NIV

Enjoy God's creation.
Play outside today.

Always be kind.

Share your faith with someone
who might not know Jesus.

THE LORD NEVER GIVES UP ON YOU;
DON'T EVER GIVE UP ON HIM.

A friend is a gift you give yourself.

ROBERT LOUIS STEVENSON

Encourage others—
Always think of others before yourself.

LOVE DOES NOT GIVE UP. LOVE IS KIND. LOVE IS
NOT JEALOUS. LOVE DOES NOT PUT ITSELF UP
AS BEING IMPORTANT. LOVE HAS NO PRIDE.
LOVE DOES NOT DO THE WRONG THING. LOVE
NEVER THINKS OF ITSELF. LOVE DOES NOT GET
ANGRY. LOVE DOES NOT REMEMBER THE SUFFERING
THAT COMES FROM BEING HURT BY SOMEONE.

1 CORINTHIANS 13:4–5 NLV

"I can't do it" never yet
accomplished anything. "I will try"
has performed wonders.

George P. Burnham

Find joy even in the small things of life.

God is your protector.
You can always rely on Him.

Encourage Others—
Really listen when someone is talking.

To accomplish great things,
we must not only act, but also dream,
not only plan, but also believe.

ANATOLE FRANCE

Never be afraid to ask for help.

IT IS A HAPPY TALENT TO
KNOW HOW TO PLAY.

RALPH WALDO EMERSON

You may be small, but you can still achieve big things.

TRUST GOD WITH ALL YOUR HEART.

Just to be is a blessing.

Your imagination is limitless.
Use it.

THE LORD DOESN'T SEE THINGS THE
WAY YOU SEE THEM. PEOPLE JUDGE BY
OUTWARD APPEARANCE, BUT THE
LORD LOOKS AT THE HEART.

1 SAMUEL 16:7 NLT

HAVE CONFIDENCE IN YOURSELF.
GOD BELIEVES IN YOU, SO YOU SHOULD, TOO!

Words can be hurtful.
Choose yours wisely.

Tomorrow is a new day.

HAPPINESS IS. . .WANTING WHAT YOU HAVE.

UNKNOWN

YOU CAN BRIGHTEN SOMEONE'S
DAY WITH A SMILE. TRY IT.

O Lord our God,
You are kind and forgiving.

DANIEL 9:9 NLV

Thank God for the beautiful
things He has given you.

BY BRINGING OUT THE BEST IN OTHERS,
YOU'LL BRING OUT THE BEST IN YOURSELF.

GOD WILL HEAL YOUR HURTS.

JUST ASK HIM.

trust God. . . .
God is our place of safety.

PSALM 62:8 CEV

Don't wait to pray.
talk to God now.

GOD MADE YOU UNIQUE.
BE PROUD OF WHO YOU ARE.

Buy a diary to write about how God has worked in your life. Read through it often to remind yourself of His goodness.

Use your talents wisely.

God knows what is deep in your heart.

IT ISN'T WHAT YOU HAVE IN YOUR
POCKET THAT MAKES YOU THANKFUL,
BUT WHAT YOU HAVE IN YOUR HEART.

UNKNOWN

A LITTLE COMPETITION IS GOOD,
BUT REMEMBER YOU DON'T HAVE TO COME
IN FIRST PLACE EVERY TIME.

thank God for something
small every day.

When a situation seems impossible,
trust in the Lord.

OPEN YOUR HEART TO THE LORD.
HE WILL LISTEN TO EVERY WORD.

SHOOT FOR THE MOON. EVEN IF YOU MISS,
YOU'LL LAND AMONG THE STARS.

LES BROWN

Be quick to forgive others.

JESUS IS AN ETERNAL LIGHT THAT WILL
SHINE EVEN ON THE DARKEST DAYS.

the love we give away is
the only love we keep.

ELBERT HUBBARD

ENCOURAGE OTHERS—
HELP A FRIEND IN NEED.

Not sure about what do do?
God will help you.

Nothing is impossible with
God by your side.

CARRY LAUGHTER WITH
YOU WHEREVER YOU GO.

HUGH SIDEY

CHILDREN, OBEY YOUR PARENTS IN EVERYTHING,
FOR THIS PLEASES THE LORD.

COLOSSIANS 3:20 NIV

God is an incredible leader.
Follow Him.

Get lost in a fun book today.

ENCOURAGE OTHERS—
COMPLIMENT SOMEONE TODAY.

GIVE THANKS TO THE LORD, FOR HE IS GOOD.
HIS LOVE ENDURES FOREVER.

PSALM 136:1 NIV

The Lord's love is never ending.

You are beautiful.

ENCOURAGE OTHERS—
DO ONE GOOD DEED EVERY DAY.

WHEN YOU FEEL ALONE, GOD IS CLOSER
THAN EVER. REACH OUT TO HIM.

Fun is good.

Dr. Seuss

Never underestimate yourself.
With God, you can do anything!

WHEN SOMEONE DOES SOMETHING
NICE FOR YOU, PASS THE KINDNESS ON.

ALWAYS LAUGH WHEN YOU CAN;
IT IS CHEAP MEDICINE. MERRIMENT IS
THE SUNNY SIDE OF EXISTENCE.

LORD BYRON

Practice makes perfect.

A friend accepts us as we are yet helps us to be what we should.

UNKNOWN

WHEN YOU ARE FILLED WITH JOY,
IT WILL SPILL OVER TO THOSE AROUND YOU.

THE BEST MINUTE YOU SPEND IS

THE ONE YOU INVEST IN SOMEONE ELSE.

UNKNOWN

Remember, it's okay to be different.

Encourage others—
Volunteer at a local organization.

GROW IN THE LOVING~FAVOR THAT
CHRIST GIVES YOU. LEARN TO KNOW OUR
LORD JESUS CHRIST BETTER. HE IS THE
ONE WHO SAVES. MAY HE HAVE ALL THE
SHINING~GREATNESS NOW AND FOREVER.

2 PETER 3:18 NLV

KEEP A CURIOUS OUTLOOK, AND YOUR LIFE

WILL BE AN AMAZING ADVENTURE.

The Lord will take all your burdens.
Just ask Him.

WORK WILLINGLY AT WHATEVER YOU DO,
AS THOUGH YOU WERE WORKING FOR THE
LORD RATHER THAN FOR PEOPLE.

COLOSSIANS 3:23 NLT

COUNT YOUR BLESSINGS ON YOUR FINGERS—

AND YOUR TOES.

Ask the Lord to be with you—

during the good times and the bad.

Stay true to the person
God created you to be.

Believe with all your heart that
God will do what He says.

GIVE ALL YOUR WORRIES AND CARES TO GOD,

FOR HE CARES ABOUT YOU.

1 PETER 5:7 NLT

ENCOURAGE OTHERS—
INVITE A SHY CLASSMATE TO SIT
WITH YOU AT LUNCH.

IF YOU DON'T UNDERSTAND

SOMETHING, ASK!

the Lord hears your prayers
and all the songs of your heart.

A SMALL COMPLIMENT OR PRAISE CAN
TURN A FROWN INTO A SMILE.
BE KIND TO SOMEONE TODAY.

"THE FEAR OF THE LORD IS THE BEGINNING
OF WISDOM, AND KNOWLEDGE OF THE
HOLY ONE IS UNDERSTANDING."

PROVERBS 9:10 NIV

Live your life for Christ.

Enjoy a sunny day at the park.

WE LOVE [JESUS], BECAUSE HE FIRST LOVED US.

1 JOHN 4:19 KJV

Read your Bible every day.
You'll be amazed how it changes your life!

A hug is a handshake from the heart.

Lending a helping hand will make you feel good and make God happy, too.

KEEP GOD AS YOUR FOCUS, AND YOU WILL
NEVER LOSE SIGHT OF HIS LOVE FOR YOU.

JUST BECAUSE EVERYONE ELSE IS DOING IT
DOESN'T MEAN YOU SHOULD DO IT, TOO.

treat others just as you
want to be treated.

Luke 6:31 CEV

BLESSED ARE THE PEACEMAKERS: FOR THEY
SHALL BE CALLED THE CHILDREN OF GOD.

MATTHEW 5:9 KJV

STAY OPTIMISTIC, NO MATTER WHAT

YOUR CIRCUMSTANCES ARE TODAY.

TOMORROW IS A NEW DAY.

YOU ARE NEVER ALONE.
GOD IS BY YOUR SIDE AND WILL HOLD
YOU CLOSE WHEN YOU NEED HIM.

YES AND *NO* ARE VERY POWERFUL WORDS.
MEAN THEM WHEN YOU SAY THEM.
RESPECT THEM WHEN YOU HEAR THEM.

MICHAEL JOSEPHSON

When you're angry,
choose your words carefully.

ENCOURAGE OTHERS—
MAKE A NEW FRIEND IN CLASS.

DON'T LET LIFE DISCOURAGE YOU;
EVERYONE WHO GOT WHERE HE IS HAD
TO BEGIN WHERE HE WAS.

RICHARD L. EVANS

trust in the Lord with all your heart.

PROVERBS 3:5 NLT

IN ORDER TO LEARN,
YOU NEED TO LISTEN FIRST.

Dream big about your future.
And then place your future
in God's hands.

GOD WILL PROVIDE EVERYTHING
YOU WILL EVER NEED. PRAISE HIM!